Also by Allan J. Cox · Confessions of a Corporate Headhunter

WORK, LOVE AND FRIENDSHIP

reflections on executive lifestyle

ALLAN J. COX

SIMON AND SCHUSTER · NEW YORK

SBN 671–27121–0
Library of Congress Catalog Card Number: 73–20699
Designed by Eve Metz
Manufactured in the United States of America

1　2　3　4　5　6　7　8　9　10

Every effort has been made to trace the ownership of all copyrighted material and to secure the necessary permission to reprint these selections. In the event of any question arising as to the use of any material, the editor and the publisher, while expressing regret for any inadvertent error, will be happy to make the necessary correction in future printings. Thanks are due to the following for permission to reprint the copyrighted material listed below:

Atheneum Publishers, for the excerpt from *The Dynamics of Creation*, by Anthony Storr, copyright © 1972 by Anthony Storr. Reprinted by permission of Atheneum.

Doubleday & Company, Inc., for the quotation from *Invitation to Sociology: A Humanistic Perspective*, by Peter L. Berger, copyright © 1963 by Peter L. Berger. An Anchor Book/Doubleday & Co., Inc.

Fortune Magazine, for the article "The Ten Highest-Ranking Women in Big Business," by Wyndham Robertson, April 1973. Courtesy of *Fortune* magazine.

Harper & Row Publishers, Inc., for the excerpt from *Reflections on the Human Condition*, by Eric Hoffer, copyright © 1973. Harper & Row.

McGraw-Hill Book Company, for the excerpt from *Culture Is Our Business*, by Marshall McLuhan, copyright © 1970 by McLuhan Associates, Ltd. Used with permission of McGraw-Hill Book Company.

Random House, Inc., for the excerpt from *The Conduct of the Corporation*, by Wilbert E. Moore, copyright © 1962. Used with permission of Random House, Inc.

Real People Press, for the quotation from *Gestalt Therapy Verbatim*, by Frederick S. Perls, copyright © 1969. Real People Press.

TO BABE

For a long time now I have been convinced that all the questions of life can be subordinated to the three major problems—the problems of communal life, of work, and of love.

—Alfred Adler

Preface

The thoughts contained in this darting volume deal with
the *as is* rather than the *ought to be*. They are reflections
on life in my world, and as such, they may not always
be appropriate for you.

As I wrote these pages I was tempted constantly to forgo
perceptions true to my lights in favor of those pointing
to a better life tomorrow. In short, it sometimes was
difficult for me to abstain from preaching what ought
to be instead of describing the here and now.

The purpose of this book is not to point to a new vision
or rally a new cause. Nor is it a positive defense of the
status quo. It is simply an attempt to offer as good-na-
turedly as possible a few insights helpful to "organization
man" concerned about the fragmentation of his life.

Allan J. Cox

I am reading Eric Hoffer's *The True Believer.* I have had it in my library for some time, knowing I would get to it sooner or later. Several years ago Eric Sevareid interviewed Hoffer on television. I liked his spontaneity and hamming; his lack of self-consciousness; his directness; his insight.

But now, halfway through the book, despite Hoffer's astute observations, I am forced again to admit that there are no answers. There are only choices in the midst of what is. What ought to be is a dead-end.

I am what I am.

You are what you are.

Sometimes my business is a pain in the neck. Sometimes I am embarrassed at how phony I am willing to be to do my job the way I think my client wants me to do it.

This is my problem; not my client's.

And the problem is my own fantasy. The client probably wishes I would stop being phony.

I alone have created the pain in my neck.

It is a quiet Saturday morning at the end of February. Bonnie has taken Laura ice skating. I am alone, sitting, sipping coffee, lazily looking out at a dirty-snow-patched Lincoln Park.

How good it feels to do nothing. To let my mind wander. To stop for a few moments or an hour to see and hear.

The park is empty. No movement. No, the stillness is movement. Very soon a defeated man with a bottle in a bag will probably come into view. Or an overly bundled toddler waddling along with mother in tow.

It is a beautiful day!

I just notice that my neck is taut. I hold it stiffly. Now that I am aware of it, I also notice that it grinds when I turn and tilt my head. God, what a sound; almost as bad as the dentist's drill.

How am I tensing myself? By making my neck stand erect on sentry duty?

What do the taut neck and erect head mean? A person afraid of making a mistake? A person holding back? I imagine so. I also suspect that the holding back is the tipoff that the sentry is not for keeping what's outside from coming in, but for keeping what's inside from coming out.

How overly seriously I take myself. What fantasies and pipe dreams I construct to kid myself into believing how important I am. What a waste of energy.

As a management consultant, or as a corporate head-hunter as I am known in some circles, I dream of power, influence and omniscience with my corporate clients. I want them to think me wise, shrewd and perceptive.

How dare they *ever* impugn my motives or question my methods! How I berate them in my mind for their inefficiencies, stupidities, superficialities and vanities.

I am entitled.

Being entitled leads to thinking myself special. Not only is this not true, but I place a great burden on my back by believing it.

Being special means I can't make mistakes.

Being special means being smartest.

Being special means having the upper hand.

Being special means I can master anything.

Being special means not admitting fears.

Being special means being right.

Being special means I cannot really listen to others.

Being special means I come first.

Being special means separating myself from my fellow man.

Being special means fighting fate when it goes against me.

Being special means self-torture guaranteed to make me feel inadequate.

Several months ago I erupted in a rage when I missed a flight that would take me to another city for what I considered a very important meeting. The new airport security procedures to prevent skyjacking were balky and slowed me down so that my plane took off without me.

That the meeting had been scheduled on a tight basis among several people only added to my helpless consternation. While lambasting airport officials for their inefficiency might have been good for release, having taken myself so seriously was not.

My thrashing over a missed flight made an impression on me. A few days later I wrote a lengthy poem to myself about how self-destructive such behavior is.

Its last stanza:

> A lesson is learned, I've a job to do,
> But force and flurry recede.
> My professional challenge must never torture
> While I'm meeting my client's need.

Jesus to his worrisome disciples:

Consider the lilies of the field, how they grow; they toil
not, neither do they spin: And yet I say unto you, That
Solomon in all his glory was not arrayed like one of these.

*

McLuhan is right. The medium is the message.

Content is less important than how it is communicated
and what it says about who is communicating.

Likewise, in business problem-solving, the process is the
solution.

Companies should look less at problems and more at
problem-solving processes.

I like Karen Horney's idea that in everything we do, we are either moving toward, away from, or against—people.

Except for Bonnie and Laura, I spend too much of my energy moving away from or against people.

I suspect this is because I like to be orderly and in control of things and people. The irony of this is that I end up being controlled by my routines and my inflexibility at meeting people on their own ground.

Controlling a relationship, whether in work or play, stifles spontaneity and play-acts facades consorting with facades.

I know that in business when I move away from or against someone, it is because I think he may harm me.

If I look into my feelings a little deeper I may discover that it is I who want to harm him and I am assuming incorrectly that he has the same designs on me. I probably telegraph my feelings without being aware of them and guarantee ill-will between us.

Often it is difficult to face up to my feelings about others. Because my goal to excel may involve my doing so at their expense, it is convenient for me to make myself believe they are my enemies. This mild form of paranoia is one of the daily rations of corporate existence.

Of course some people pattern their lives for destructive-
ness. I would be foolish not to defend against or avoid
such onslaughts.

And others with sincerity and good intentions hold views
and seek courses of action which run counter to what I
value. This cannot be helped. It is part of living in a
complex world. The important thing is to spend my energy
on those things I value and to be open to move toward
others who share those values.

I am reminded of Fritz Perls' credo:

I do my thing, and you do your thing.
I am not in this world to live up to your expectations.
And you are not in this world to live up to mine.
You are you and I am I.
And if by chance we find each other, it's beautiful.
If not, it can't be helped.

I cannot *make* anyone like me.

I can only be likable.

And I can only be likable to certain people, not all people.

How much easier my life would be if I would simply give up the nonsense of wanting to be loved by everybody.

*

*

Some people make big promises.

Others offer elaborate descriptions of what they are going to do.

I listen to people's words less than I watch their feet.

The more I talk about doing something, the less chance there is that I will ever do it.

If I truly understand what a person is doing, I don't have to ask him what his feelings are.

A person *is* what he *does*.

✳

*

The most important time is *now.*

The future is life's abductor. By focusing my consciousness on tomorrow's goals, I rob myself of being responsive to today.

While looking ahead, I am not seeing, hearing, touching, tasting and smelling opportunities that are all around me now.

Planning—corporate or personal—is not unimportant, but it is overrated.

Fortune ran an article
in April 1973:

THE TEN
HIGHEST-RANKING
WOMEN
IN BIG BUSINESS

Catherine Cleary was one of them . . .

Catherine Cleary

"I hope someone hasn't told you she thinks like a man," says a long-time business associate of Catherine Cleary, "because Catherine just *thinks.*" Miss Cleary, fifty-six, an outgoing woman with a keen sense of humor, is president of First Wisconsin Trust Co. (assets under management: $1.25 billion). *"I've never had a plan,"* says Miss Cleary, who once had a passing yen to be in the theatre and taught school for a while before deciding to become a lawyer. After a few years of law practice, she moved, at thirty-one, to the trust company. She rose steadily through trust administration (rather than the investment side of the business) and was named chief executive officer in 1970. Since she took over, the company's earnings have risen sharply. *"If I had any sense,"* she says, *"I'd quit right now."* She is a member of the board of First Wisconsin Bankshares, parent to the trust company, and of four other corporate giants: A.T.&T., General Motors, Kraftco, and Northwestern Mutual Life Insurance Co. (of which her father was once the president). These boards, and the board committees she sits on, hold over fifty meetings a year, so Miss Cleary sees a lot of the Milwaukee airport.

Young adults today are more in touch with the now. They wisely seek de-emphasis of goals and involvement *in* roles.

They know that in a very real sense the future belongs to those who don't prepare for it.

*

✳

Alfred Adler was the first to use the term *Life Style*. He made it an integral part of his theory of personality. Today, the term has been popularized and means different things to different people.

To Adler, *Life Style* is simply an organized set of convictions about life. That's what it means to me and how I use it in these pages.

There are healthy and non-healthy lifestyles.

There are self-enhancing and self-limiting lifestyles.

To talk about executive lifestyle is cheating, because a set of convictions about life extends to more than one's career.

But you know this already—that I am emphasizing how we in the executive world are as concerned about a self-enhancing lifestyle as anyone else.

The first step I can take in moving toward a self-enhancing lifestyle is to realize that I am embarking on a journey; a pilgrimage.

The path will be long and winding, leading to places I cannot and do not wish to anticipate lest I miss the joys of discovery in the here and now.

What I will discover, starting right now, is bits and pieces of who I am.

I am not somebody else. I am who I am.

I am not something else. I am what I am.

To start with, I am . . .
    competitive
    impulsive
    intelligent
    overweight
    fickle
    capable
    proud
    perceptive
    organized
    jealous
    lazy
    thin-skinned
    begrudging
    manipulative
    anxious
    aggressive
    sometimes shy
    supportive
    self-conscious
    a good listener
    easily discouraged
    and a thousand other things, "good" and "bad"

I am becoming more at ease with who I am. This does not mean I will rest on my laurels, some of which are indeed questionable. Or to put it another way, this does not mean that I do not need to change, or that I cannot change.

But it does mean I will torture myself less when needed change comes about slowly.

And discover that, on balance, I'm not such a bad guy.

And that what I am is in some ways unique; creative; even brilliant!

That which is unique and worthwhile in us makes itself felt in flashes. If we do not know how to catch and savor the flashes we are without growth and without exhilaration.
—Eric Hoffer

Real change in my personality will come about spontaneously.

It will come about through my own discovery.

Sometimes I think that I can't *make* myself do anything; that everything I do I do because I want to do it; even when I claim I don't want to do it.

Often what passes for change in my personality is simply part of the real me I've just discovered.

It has existed all along, but I have kept it encased in my emotional armor where even I had no access to it.

When Saul became St. Paul, did he change?

*

*

I want very much to succeed in business.

But I do not want to succeed at the expense of not being an authentic person.

I have to mesh who I am with what the corporation is.

One essential in doing this is to see the corporation as it is, not as it is supposed to be, or portrayed to be.

I have to see behind the corporate facades.

Hyperbole is the language of business.

Advertising is shouting just to be heard.

Corporate objectives are homilies.

Job descriptions keep the forest products industry healthy by using paper.

Stated achievements are interpretation.

Quantitative data are history.

The rhetoric of rational management is fiction-diction.

One facade of the corporation is its rhetoric about rationality.

This is hardly a novel thought.

But it is an irritating one to those who would have us believe that the language in annual reports and public statements by corporate leaders accurately conveys how a company conducts its daily business.

In all manner of media we are reminded that companies

plan
  strategize
    implement
      execute
        phase out
          phase in
            diversify
              acquire
              divest
              hire
                fire
                  research
                  develop

It is implicit in such press that these cerebral and motor activities are carried out in accordance with an all-encompassing, explicit scheme.

Companies install elaborate financial controls with detailed procedures for budgeting. They put their most analytical executives to work in corporate planning.

The planning department itself is headed by a vice president who is a specialist in corporate planning. He might well have attended seminars at Stanford Research to enhance his credentials.

His job is to produce six-month, one-year, five-year and ten-year plans. He also formulates new product, diversification, merger and acquisition plans.

Most important, he produces contingency plans, one of which is a career plan that becomes operative when things don't go according to plan.

Inventories are controlled. Production is controlled. Value engineering is installed. PERT charts are drawn. Divisional performance and reporting procedures are monitored. Departments are constructed as profit centers so they can be held accountable.

Management-by-objectives is installed so executive performance can be measured. Training seminars are held so managers can be channeled properly. Market research grows more sophisticated.

Organization charts are drafted and modified with bold lines, thin lines, dotted lines, participating-interlinking groups and matrixes of reporting relationships. Detailed, lengthy job descriptions abound. The management grid surveys all, and theory Y keeps everybody happy.

Not only is it a marvel that such controls exist, but also that the state of effectiveness and deliverance of promise of an entire corporation, or any of its "modules," can be measured and reproduced mathematically!

The regenerative conduit of such life-giving information emanates from the central nervous system of the corporate body: the computer.

But these rational procedures rely on people for enactment.

And people often are more irrational than they are rational.

The neat little boxes in the latest organization chart represent people who face their corporate responsibilities with varying degrees of commitment.

One executive recently promoted to his job is enthusiastic. Another recently passed over is hostile. Another is elated that his son has been accepted at Princeton.

One executive smiles at his boss, agrees with everything he says, and covertly looks for another job because he can't stand his guts.

Still another receives test results from his physician and learns that his "heart murmurs" are serious.

Two executives in R&D are furious that their new product ideas are turned down and go into business for themselves.

These examples illustrate that companies are controlled by irrational forces as much as by rational ones.

Knowing the organization chart does not guarantee knowing the organization.

And ignoring the fact that individuals often behave irrationally in corporations because they are meeting their personal needs is to foreclose any attempt to harmonize organization and human objectives.

*

*

I am not fond of big-talking men making
   big deals smoking big cigars
      in little elevators.

Nothing annoys me more than being talked
   to over the speaker-phone when
      it is unnecessary.

*

Passivity is an attitude I find offensive in others. In executives it often takes the form of . . .

"What should I do now?"

"The circumstances were beyond my control."

"Oh, I never expected that."

"But you didn't tell me I was supposed to do that."

"Fat chance that could ever happen."

"Everything is going against me."

"I wish I had been aware of that."

"I told you so."

Passivity is like shyness. It is an attempt to make others come to you.

It is designed to put others into your service.

It is avoiding taking a chance.

It is a guarantee of not making a mistake.

It is evading responsibility.

It is probable that I dislike passivity because I fear it in myself.

But my method of dealing with passivity is to fly into the face of it.

If my suspicion is correct, that underneath I am as afraid of failure as anyone else, I am satisfied with the way I choose to cope with it.

Today a very talented friend is coming for advice on his career. Initially, I was annoyed because I thought he was being passive. "You have a better brain and are even more ambitious than me. Work it out yourself, man."

As I thought about his wanting to talk, it dawned on me that he wasn't being passive at all. This fellow is narcissistic and likes attention.

Now that I have figured out the game, I can give him his strokes ungrudgingly. And I can enjoy his coming to me for help.

But I am betting he will be late for our appointment.

I was right. He was late for the appointment.

*

There is a rhythm in my work, as there is in most things. If I am sensitive to the people and situation around me, I can flow with the rhythm and accomplish much more with less effort.

Often, when I try to speed things up, it develops that I slow them down.

When I force people (including myself) to do things that don't fit the rhythm, I eventually discover that I have been attempting to meet some illegitimate "need" rather than getting the job done.

Judgment and timing in proper combination seem to be the qualities most critical to success in business.

They are more critical than ability.

They are more critical than education.

They are more critical than training.

They are more critical than experience.

They are more critical than intelligence.

They are more critical than sincerity.

They are more critical than drive.

Judgment and timing cannot be measured.

They can only be observed.

✳

*

There are three stages of the typical family-held company.

They parallel the three generations of father, son and grandson.

Thunder

Wonder

Plunder

*

65

*

Getting down to the nitty-gritty, I sometimes think life, despite its embellishments, is made up of vested interests and rationalizations.

The vested interest comes first.

The rationalization follows.

The social nature of man would discredit the witnesses for this indictment, but the perversity of human nature testifies on its behalf.

*

*

Despite earlier intentions to the contrary, I have learned that it is impossible to survive the rigors of a business career with the mind of an angel.

What is required for running the race while balancing my psyche is the skillful blending of . . .

   genial skepticism about corporate objectives

   a good-humored but ruthless commitment
   to my career

   a sanguine view of the perversity of human nature

Such attitudes are deplorable to the new breed of organization development specialists.

Their belief in "human relations" management runs counter to such convictions.

While I agree with their principles, and hope that what they preach becomes a reality, I notice they are very competitive with each other when thrown together to do a job.

In business,

malevolent

is not

irrelevant.

Today I worked on a project with a polite but uncommitted man.

While growing impatient with his lack of involvement, I learned that our interests in what should come out of this project were diametrically opposed.

There is more to conflict than the emotional elements. There is the competition for rewards assumed to be scarce.

Conflict *resolution* for all cases is an illusion.
Conflict *management* for many cases is all that can be hoped for.

Interpersonal conflict that does not attack
the philosophical roots of a company
actually can be helpful.

It may lead to a realignment of power more in
keeping with working relationships as
they truly exist.

But conflict where rivals no longer agree on
the philosophical roots may tear a
company apart.

A funny thing about closely knit groups:

They can be short-lived.

In their intensity of commitment to a task, they exact a selflessness from their members.

Individual feelings and needs are subordinated to the will of the group.

Ill-will is suppressed.

When conflict will no longer be denied, it explodes.

The group disintegrates.

Closely knit groups often have charismatic leaders.

I wonder if charismatic leaders are short-termers.

Are they always moving on?

Mayor Daley is not charismatic.

J. Edgar Hoover was not charismatic.

In the loosely knit group, conflict is more common but less destructive.

Personalities are not subordinated to the will of the group.

The more numerous but less intense conflicts prevent the group from dividing over any one.

The moral: intensity of conflict is inversely related to its frequency and diversity.

Conflict as such does not threaten the equilibrium of a company.

Rigidity is the culprit.

Unwillingness to permit expression of negative feelings guarantees a drawn battle-line.

When conflict erupts, company stability is threatened.

❋

*

The paradox of human nature is that while I need my fellow man and seek to be near him, I want to feel superior to him.

I notice that the possibilities for my most consistently resolving this paradox exist in my marriage.

I cannot resolve the paradox without experiencing pain, for those qualities I most genuinely love in Bonnie can also hurt me deeply.

I love her for her . . .

irreverence

quietness—for being silent when she has nothing
to say

privateness with strangers and phonies

selfishness—for preserving her *self* and, thereby, her
authenticity

fire and grudges

judgment and insight

I also love her . . .

for showing me that I am not an extrovert

for not indulging my impulses

for showing me that love is *never* unconditional

And for all the traditional things:

for her support when I am discouraged

for her prettiness

for her motherliness to Laura

for her need of my protectiveness

for her indecisiveness in her own life

for her need of my love

I—THOU

I've cheated you by cheating me
Fearful of your scornful glances
Waiting for OK, OK
To make me sweet, make me loving
Acted on instead of acting

No eyes of my own, only looked upon
Being seen, never seeing
Who am I, the great nobody
Known by all, knowing no one
Getting hurt and hurting you

Empty faces, arid fields
Peopleless dreams, riverless mountains
Signs of the times, talk without feeling
Concrete cities, plastic flowers
Lives without breathing

I come to you, I want to
You find yours, I find mine
We meet again without leeching
We love new and live fresh
And claim what is ours, ours alone

We pay our dues
But the dues aren't dues
In pain there's growth
You're mine because you're you
I'm yours because I'm me

How the world comes alive, now the rivers dance
I see *you,* you're not my mirror
No more fears for scornful glances
You're my love!
It is exciting, exciting

✳

In the past three or four years I have encountered growing disenchantment among executives with "the system."
As a confidant to executives I work with, I am privy to
some of their most candid emotions.

An increasing number are becoming more openly vocal
about what they consider dehumanizing in corporate life.

Discontent among workers has been prevalent since the
days of the Industrial Revolution, but the disaffection of
the well-paid executive is something new. Executive drop-
out, even among those doing well, is no longer a rare
occurrence.

Some of the reasons executives give for dropping out seem superficial, an avoidance of responsibility based on a world-view which is narrow rather than broad.

Their movement is often a flight from rather than a flight to.

But I see this movement as the tip of the iceberg, the sign of a deeper humanistic evolution going on in the corporate world.

Whether radical or reactionary, today's super-alarmists are frightened pitchmen with no sense of history.

The major advances in civilization are processes that all but wreck the societies in which they occur.
—Alfred North Whitehead

Toleration of the anxiety caused by chaos is one characteristic of the creative person, who must be prepared to see his grasp of the world broken before he can renew it.
—Anthony Storr

✳

When it comes to gut decisions, I know that logic is a joke.

I am embarrassed at how many times I have approached
a tough decision by taking a blank sheet of paper, drawing
a line down the middle and listing the pros and cons on
either side of the line, but finally listening to my stomach
for the answer.

My embarrassment is not for listening to my stomach, but
for going through the silly exercise with the paper.

Many times I ask the question *why* when knowing the *how* would teach me a method while answering the *why.* For example, if I ask a vice president of sales how he divides up his national sales force, if I am using my brain at all, I will also, in the process, learn why he divides it up that way.

Why is content and intellectual and thinking.

How is process and action and doing.

My business experience teaches me that usually I can capture the former by paying attention to the latter.

At least as far as my job is concerned, the *whys* more often than not are irrelevant to the problem at hand.

How was this decision made is usually a more revealing question than why was it made.

How did this problem come to your attention is usually more revealing than why did it come to your attention.

How was this problem reformulated is usually more revealing than why was it reformulated.

How do you train new management recruits is usually more revealing than why do you train them.

How are committee members selected is usually more revealing than why are they selected.

How deals with structure and function.

Why often deals with rhetoric and fantasy.

✳

*

I often use questions not to get answers at all, but to keep obnoxious executives at bay.

You might want to play this game sometime: see how long you can keep a compulsive talker going with no responses from you except changing facial expressions, occasional nodding and periodic monosyllables.

I enjoy my rather advanced skill in this area. It is a great defense against one of the occupational hazards of my profession.

And I use this otherwise idle time for what's really on my mind.

Some of my best thinking has been done while others are talking.

*

There are times to be vulnerable and times not to be vulnerable.

With my friends and my wife I am willing to be vulnerable. In business I am seldom willing to be so.

I sometimes play-act vulnerability in business by confessing to everything but the truth. I am seldom caught.

*

Robert Merton has given us the terminology of *manifest* and *latent* functions.

Manifest functions are those which are given rhetorical consensus and sanction. They are the generally believed purposes for which a building is built, a foundation is formed, a business is started or a couple has three children.

Latent functions are the underlying and usually unconscious bases for action being taken and for things being as they are.

Manifest functions are the *whys.*

Latent functions are the *hows.*

Manifest functions are up front.

Latent functions are down below.

Manifest functions are the facade.

Latent functions are the substance.

The manifest function of the new president reorganizing the company is to make it more efficient while cutting costs.

The latent function may be to establish his authority while portraying him as a man of action.

The manifest function of establishing a management-by-objectives program is to motivate executives through increased participation.

The latent function may be to enhance top management's reputation for being progressive.

The manifest function of conventions and trade shows is to keep industry members up-to-date on trends and developments.

The latent function may be to provide a vehicle for keeping up with industry contacts when members need to change jobs.

The manifest function of the annual performance appraisal is to provide for an objective evaluation of executive achievement and a basis for future training.

The latent function is to encourage a political climate in which subordinates curry favor with their bosses because they know there is no way such appraisals can be objective.

When a president or another senior member of management wants my assistance or advice in a project or program he has announced or is contemplating, I always look for the latent functions.

Sometimes my major contribution is pointing out the latent functions of a program. It is not necessarily that the client is insincere, but that he may be too close to the situation to see them himself.

Other clients may be close-minded and want to believe the manifest functions, but they are nonetheless governed by the latent ones.

These are dangerous situations for me. They require speaking with a forked tongue while feigning sincere devotion to the official dogma. Learning to do this has been the most critical factor in ensuring my survival in corporate life.

The major institutions of our society, including the economic one, have values and a wisdom of their own.

They are expressed in their latent functions.

*

*

When I am able to put myself in my adversary's shoes, I can understand his behavior against me with less difficulty. In time, if not right away, I even may be able to develop a sense of humor about our jousting.

It is also true that only when I have come to terms with myself and my numerous roles in society will I be constructively dispassionate about my world.

Peter Berger, the witty, brilliant sociologist, captures better than anyone I know how we can fulfill our roles meaningfully in society without taking it all too seriously.

"Another option is what we regard as the most plausible . . . one that can combine compassion, limited commitment and a sense of the comic in man's social carnival.

"This will lead to a posture vis-à-vis society based on a perception of the latter as essentially a comedy, in which men parade up and down with their gaudy costumes, change hats and titles, hit each other with the sticks they have or the ones they can persuade their fellow actors to believe in.

". . . If one views society as a comedy, one will not hesi-
tate to cheat, especially if by cheating one can alleviate a
little pain here or make life a little brighter there. One will
refuse to take seriously the rules of the game, except
insofar as these rules protect real human beings and
foster real human values.

"Sociological Machiavellianism is thus the very opposite of cynical opportunism. It is the way in which freedom can realize itself in social action."

✳

Today, for the thousandth time, I listened to a well-edu-
cated, experienced, 50-year-old executive recount that
he feels his corporation no longer values his services.

It seems that the half-century mark, give or take a year or
two, has become an unprogrammed time for an executive
to take a new look at himself, and for his corporation to
do the same.

The hard truth is that the companies feel fewer pangs of
conscience cutting off a man at this time than they would
a few years later.

The executive takes stock anew because he can no longer
deny to himself that he is on the downside of life. He has
new zeal to make the remaining years of his career as
enjoyable as possible.

Sometimes companies are on a youth-kick and give a perfectly splendid executive short shrift.

Sometimes the executive, with his zeal for enriching his later years, suddenly becomes unhappy at 50 with the job he was content with at 49. He precipitates a problem for himself by making demands on his company that cannot be met, or at least not as quickly as he wants.

Sadly, sometimes the executive has *not* kept up with the times, has not remained fresh in spirit and has fallen into a rut.

When I listen to a man discuss ways of charting a new, stimulating course for the rest of his working life, I get excited.

And when I listen to a man who is a victim of a corporate youth-kick, a merger or a reorganization, I can be supportive.

But when I hear a man blame others and circumstance for a plight which has resulted from his own obliviousness, dullness and passivity, I have no patience.

Thinking of age reminds me of people who live their lives on the basis of probabilities.

They see themselves not as people but as statistics.

People who are concerned with chronological age, and with themselves as probability statistics, will go through life feeling either too old or too young.

People who do distinctive things don't think probabilities.

They go for the jugular.

*

Have you ever noticed how carrying an attaché case keeps you from walking properly?

You cannot swing your arms, but instead must walk with your arm hanging by your side, stoop-shouldered, like a gorilla.

With proper training over the years, I may be able to scratch my left knee without bending at the waist.

My posture tells me things about myself that my mind is unwilling to admit.

When I lean against the wall of an elevator, or a doorway, I am reminded that far too often I do not stand on my own two feet.

As I lean forward when walking, my normal gait, I am reminded that my basic thrust in life is a bit too angry. But the bounce in my step tells me that I do what I do with a basic rhythm.

My slouching in chairs reminds me that I am too dependent on others for approval.

My animated, gesturing arms tell me I am willing to communicate openly with those around me.

My crossed arms tell me that I am not.

My crossed perspiring hands tell me I'd rather be pounding my fist on the table. The man across the table needn't know that, but it's important that I do.

My pointing finger says, "Listen here, that's the way it's gonna be!"

My waving finger says, "You're one devious operator, mister."

*

Executives I see on the street whom I've met, who don't see me, aren't ignoring me. But they're showing me the main thrust of their lifestyle and how they relate to most people.

They are moving away. By their behavior they are saying, "I'm special. If you want to know me, you'll have to come to me, not just this time, but again and again."

They are not risk-takers, but are afraid of failure and rejection. And I am willing to bet these qualities will show up in the way they approach their jobs.

Executives with stunted powers of observation are telling me that they are more bent on *not* knowing than they are on growing.

They are not innovators and miss opportunities others see in abundance.

*

*

I encounter self-limiting, defensive, executive lifestyles
daily. I spot them with an eye whose acuteness has been
nurtured by fees my clients pay me to be right.

Smugly basing decisions on "types" is fraught with pit-falls: all generalizations will eventually present their notable exceptions to stand up and smite me uncere-moniously.

But while I am watchful for the man whose individual pattern defies ordinary predictability, such surprises are few among the following breeds of corporate pretenders:

THE NARCISSIST: needs to be loved . . . thrives on being the object of attention of his subordinates . . . is overly sensitive and easily offended . . . usually dresses fastidiously, in the latest fashion . . . often uses his first initial and second name, such as E. Arthur Hartwell . . . after all, he couldn't go through life simply as "Ed." Have you ever noticed how many corporate presidents use their first initial and second name? . . . Initials say nothing of ability, but they speak volumes of how a man sees himself.

THE ADVERSARY: thrives on conflict . . . turns every business conversation and decision-making situation into a power struggle . . . more negative than the devil's advocate, he gets abusive . . . holds grudges . . . always has a frown on his face.

THE DIPLOMAT: the exact opposite of the adversary . . . conflict gives him sweaty palms and hemorrhoids . . . soft-spoken and smooth . . . nice-guy image . . . will tell lies if necessary to avoid unpleasant confrontations . . . beware his annual review of your performance if he's your boss.

THE ABRASIVE: different from the adversary . . . usually smarter and more talented . . . lacks finesse to move up to top management because he lacks people skills and often has parochial interests . . . if he can be lived with he is often valuable to the company . . . but he does cause trouble.

THE SALESMAN: the master of double talk and diversion . . . his charm and persuasion often distract his listeners from his empty head and lack of administrative prowess . . . not to be confused with sales executives . . . an absolute menace.

THE PROFESSOR: the learned lecturer . . . likes to call meetings at which he conducts lengthy discourses, and answers questions nobody has asked . . . will not tolerate interruptions, but after the meeting expects to be commended for his analytical ability . . . stopping by his office at 5 P.M. guarantees a missed commuter train.

THE GOSSIP: everyone knows this fellow . . . his long nose rests squarely in the crotch of the grapevine . . . nothing personal or impersonal relating to anybody escapes his attention . . . usually holds an unimportant job or wouldn't have time for his exhaustive reconnaissance activities.

THE DETAILER: becomes so mired in minutiae that he is ineffective . . . his self-foil is that he has conned himself into believing he is the only person who can do any number of trivial jobs right . . . cannot bring himself to delegate responsibility or authority.

THE OVER-DELEGATER: the opposite of the detailer . . . his slogan is "It's your baby" . . . sloppy in his work habits . . . doesn't stay on top of anything . . . lacks follow-through, stick-to-itiveness . . . characterized by disjointedness and half-hearted efforts on grapeshot projects . . . his gyrating antenna guarantees dissonance.

THE SPRINTER: off the starting block with a flash, but he trips over the second hurdle and is out of the race . . . lacks endurance.

THE BLUEBLOOD: depends on social snobbery, an Ivy League degree and family connections to get him through . . . all kinds of beautiful exceptions, of course, but these inadequate types still abound.

THE ETHNIC HOUND: this fellow's father was an hourly worker, lived in a basement apartment, didn't own a car and rode his bicycle to the Savings & Loan every Saturday morning to make his deposit . . . is a graduate of a state university, but social mobility notwithstanding, has difficulty shaking his upbringing . . . is thrifty and will make somebody one hell of an engineer, plant manager or controller . . . but he usually can't see the big picture.

THE GRAND EXECUTOR: believes in bold strategies . . . as long as they're on paper . . . he's planning an invasion of Normandy, but he'll never get his ships out of his own harbor . . . lots of smoke, no fire . . . two years after joining the company, everyone is still waiting for him to make his big move.

THE GRAND INTERPRETER: doesn't believe in verbal economies . . . whether writing or talking, always uses three words when one will do . . . in conversation, modifies and feeds back what you've said using his verbal multiplier . . . if you call yourself a paint salesman, he'll call you a means-ends deliverance system to the ecological-epidermal market.

THE PRIME-TIME LEECH: because of laziness, loneliness or not having enough to do, waltzes into your office with regularity and asks, "Have you got a minute?" . . . keeps you from getting your work done while seeking your advice on matters where he hasn't the least intention of applying your counsel, if you've been silly enough to give it . . . he's surprised when he's the first to go in a management cutback.

THE FRENETIC: this is the busy man . . . his schedule is a never-ending whirlwind of appointments, projects, due dates, phone calls, travels . . . ends up late for appointments, fouls up projects, misses due dates, too busy to take phone calls or return them, and delays travel plans . . . his mode is hurrying, scurrying, worrying.

THE DOWN-HOME SCHEMER: this is the guy with an angle . . . makes the bargain he wants to strike with you sound plausible, as if he's watching out for your interests in the company . . . you're not sure why, but you know he's on the con . . . you count your fingers after you shake hands with him . . . if you avoid him you find out soon enough what he was after—and the interests he was watching were his own . . . he's the street merchant gone executive suite.

THE SOFT-SHOE HOOFER: the cleverest of the corporate deviants . . . difficult to get him to take a stand on anything : . . if you try to pin him down and hold him to something he has said, he'll say you misinterpreted him . . . not transparent in his self-serving like the salesman . . . bright . . . understands the nuances of language and can talk himself out of any jam . . . defuses criticisms of his actions by making fun of himself, confessing to everything but the truth . . . simulates warmth . . . convinces all, sometimes himself, of his sincerity . . . usually has longevity in the company and has had his share of promotions . . . only the unusually perceptive can spot him.

*

Robert Townsend is right.

Most corporate staff services should go.

Good presidents *do* carry watermelons at the company picnic.

I have noticed that senior executives are no more immune to intellectual faddism than anyone else.

When ideologies claimed to be appropriate for business are presented as new knowledge it will pay to examine them for traces of false consciousness and propaganda.

The organization development movement strikes me as one deserving such scrutiny.

Its hope and promise are heartening.

But the claims and the conditions required for success by its practitioners are propaganda.

To say the very least, their expectations are wishful thinking.

While the goals of organizational development are laudable, desired results from its typical brand of behavioral science methods require the environmental support characteristic of most clinical settings.

Expecting such support from a majority of executives in a setting that is clearly not clinical, but economic, is nonsense.

The perversity of human nature, the self interests in making one's own living, and the mobility of executives—geographically and vertically—will destroy the cooperative interpersonal webwork necessary to make organizational development methods work over time.

Certainly no irreparable harm ever comes from business welcoming a new panacea with open arms.

The idealism and enthusiasm distract and ameliorate for a time.

And no one can dispute that any inching ahead in human relations is a good thing.

But even where top management is not expecting miracles and has the courage to experiment with progressive methods, there are so few executives who are willing to be fully human, to take the risks necessary to grow.

Most management development is
corporate entertainment.

But human development
for executives
isn't.

It seems more and more likely that corporations will encourage human development among their enlightened, emotionally secure executives.

If carried out properly, a corporation's focus for human development will not be to make better managers of its men, *but better men of its managers.*

Executive-as-human is the new paradigm . . . at least among those who are effective.

*

If you agree with me that life is often little more than
vested interest and rationalization, the first question you
must always ask is:

SAYS WHO?

I am always more interested in dealing with someone who can show me how something is done than with the person who can tell me how to do it.

There are inarticulate doers and articulate teachers.

I would rather watch a doer than listen to a teacher.

*

I marvel at how much I misuse my faculties for defensive purposes.

For example, there seems to be no limit to my creativity in remaking history through my memory.

And then there is the matter of bogus friendship . . .

In the past, I have trapped myself into pretended friend-
ships. These were relationships I fostered for illegitimate
purposes centering on two areas where I wanted support.
The first was companionships to reinforce my tentative
beliefs that I was "well liked." The second was advance-
ment in my career. Both were carried out under my
illusion of extroversion—that I thrived on people and
wanted to be around them.

These pseudo-friendships were parasitic in outlook and
fruitless in outcome. They could be none other because
they were designed to make me feel superior to those
I was putting into my service.

In the process, I learned a valuable lesson: anyone who
was passive enough to let me seek fulfillment of my needs
on such an illegitimate basis soon would grow to dislike
me, even if he couldn't admit it to himself.

There is a gray area of self-interest in which I must stay if I am to be able to be friends with someone. If a relationship smothers my needs, I will turn on the one whom I am allowing to limit my freedom.

When I find myself cornered this way, I usually discover that I have been playing the shy game or am fearful of offending the other person.

What a ridiculous game: if not asserting myself allows the other person to like me (whatever his reasons), it will be the me *I* don't like.

It is not the other person's responsibility to *let* me be me. It is my responsibility to look after myself and stand on my own two feet.

Ours is an ambiguous complex world presenting many choices.

It is inevitable that sometimes your and my choices will be in conflict.

It will go better for us if we are not apologetic about those choices.

Cooperation can exist without friendship, but friendship cannot exist without cooperation.

In the community, cooperation tends to be articulated: we agree to share the water supply.

In friendship, cooperation often escalates to non-verbal forms: without telling you or even thinking about it, I may let you have some of my water.

Most of what passes for cooperation is really accommodation.

In friendship accommodation is alien.

Friendship is based more on shared values than changed ones.

I influence my friends and they influence me.

But our friendship is founded much more in what we share than in how we might change each other.

*

I have faced the fact that a friend may not always remain a friend.

Whether I am comfortable with the notion or not, as my values change, so will some of my friends.

It makes sense to travel light not only materially, but ideologically as well.

Though it is theoretically possible to work through any relationship, no matter how rocky its beginning, I don't obligate myself to do so.

More than once, when circumstances would not be denied, I found a friend who was cloaked originally as an enemy. I am happy for those occasions, but I don't go looking for them.

No longer an extrovert, I now prefer to closet myself with my family and share my biases, tastes, habits, joys and discouragements with a few close friends who like what I give and give what I like.

✳

Today we received Laura's semi-annual review from her teacher. The entire three-page report is gratifying, but one comment in particular makes me very happy:

"Laura's beautiful originality and expressiveness in art and music reflect the joy which pervades her approach to life."

Laura is joy

Joy is exciting

Exciting is Laura

At seven, Laura now seems so grown up, so delightfully mischievous, good-humored, fearless, positive and charming. She also has a strong temper, but that doesn't bother me. She's alive!

When I think of that ugly infant with the red face and squashed nose, whose incessant crying made us feel so inadequate, who spit up at one end and filled her diapers at the other, I can't believe her new-found combination of purposefulness and subtlety.

*

I notice lately that I get most angry at Bonnie for not playing my straight man; for not encouraging me when I try to convince both of us of something I myself do not believe.

The more she denies me, the more grand and bizarre my monologues become.

Will it always take a night's sleep for me to discover what she knew all along?

I am in New York City on a business trip. I am sitting in my room at the Lombardy, my favorite hotel. I have an hour to kill before my next appointment. It is a freakishly warm day in early March. The temperature is in the seventies. I am ruminating. My ruminations fit the patterns of spring fever.

I remember my comments about Bonnie and that usually she will not let me get away with false doctrine. I wonder what false doctrines I believe that I have not shared with her; that I have not even faced myself because I know that to face them is to puncture them, and I am not ready for that yet.

I wonder if I will always be a headhunter. The thought makes me shudder because I don't like to think I will *always* be anything. I am a vocational claustrophobic. Now I realize that I am torturing myself with the future, trying to map out and control again, sitting in a hotel room having stupid thoughts when I should be outside walking around enjoying the NOW, this beautiful day.

An hour to *kill?*

Of course I am not a headhunter. I am a headhunter
AND. . . .

I am a headhunter *and* the youngest child in a
   family of four.
   and a former college instructor.
   and a former high school athlete.
   and a man who hates to shine his shoes.
   and a person who likes to get to the airport
      at least fifteen minutes before the plane leaves.
   and a writer of sorts.
   and a poet of sorts.
   and one who likes to go to bed early.
   and a man who often is inconsiderate
      to his wife and daughter.
   and a man who craves pasta and thinks German
      white wines better than French.
   and a man who is erratic in the quality of his
      speeches, but is good at answering questions
      after the speech.
   and etc., etc., etc.

I like to remind myself that I am many things, many-faceted; that I am not a role, or even many roles.

I am a *person.*

I *play* roles.

I am a person who sometimes plays the role of head-hunter.

I am what I do.

Playing a role is doing.

I am a role?

Not so!
Awareness is doing.
I can be aware I am playing.

I am a person.
A person who is aware.

Bureaucracy fragments.

Awareness integrates.

Being trapped by a role means that in my self-view I have become indistinguishable from the role.

As long as I realize that I am not a role, but am merely playing one, I won't be trapped by it.

I will not always be able to choose my roles, but I can choose to be aware that I am playing them.

And since role performance is usually open to interpretation, I have leeway in how I will play mine. And if I go a step further in my awareness, I will also give thought to how I want to *appear* to be playing my role.

Playing the role of headhunter does not exempt me from producing results for corporate managements who have come to me for help.

But the role of headhunter has many sub-roles affording me many options. If I will be alive to circumstances unfolding all around me, if I will free my imagination, I will discover new ways to shape this abstraction called a role.

And when, for the sake of my survival, I cannot escape the more comic elements of role-playing, I can buttress my sanity by laughing at the performance I feel required to give.

Most of the executives with whom I deal on a daily basis cannot see themselves apart from their vocational role.

Impressive, disciplined and committed, they are hell-bent in the race to the finish.

Not until exhaustion or shameful defeat interrupts can they bring themselves to contemplate an alternative lifestyle and an alternative way of playing their vocational role.

THE MIGHTY MEN

Grapplers, runners, Hercules awesome
Men of action, unquenched rigor
Toil unending, training and striving
Their vision blurred save final goal
The race is on, all pain denied

Singleminded, determined fighters
Buffeting, careening
The chariot-like rhythm
Mesmerizes and sways
The race is on, all pain denied

Nagging fears, fatigue sneaking
Tightened stomach and clenched fists
Whip new thrust, rechannel vision
The goal returns
The race is on, all pain denied

Sweet victory grows amorphous
Exhaustion lifts blindness
Open sky intrudes the track
The race is on, but just one victor
Pain says it won't be you

Grapplers, runners, Hercules awesome
Men of action, unquenched rigor
What race is this? Just one victor!
The collective pain spits on the goal
And teaches it is life's abductor.

✳

*

I do not try to be the best, but rather the most appropriate, in whatever I do.

I am not an absolutist, but a relativist.

I believe in contexts.

To try to be best is to condemn myself to the curse of perfectionism.

✱

Some executives have little concept of time. Whether their project stretches over weeks, months or simply an afternoon, they dramatically misjudge how long that project will take to complete.

I have never met a truly effective executive who suffered from this problem.

Other executives habitually are late for appointments.

That is a different problem stemming not from busyness or disorganization but from submerged narcissism and power-seeking.

When you are kept waiting by someone, that person has placed himself at the center of your attention.

And if habitually he makes you wait for him, he enjoys your subservience.

*

*

Tonight when I first got home I was hyped up. I had kept a frenetic pace during the day, but besides that, a very important meeting took place between a client and candidate this afternoon and I won't learn the results of the meeting until tomorrow.

I thought of calling my client at home and then began to regain my perspective. Absolutely not! Tonight is now, and now is for relaxing.

Emotional overinvestment in one's career is always a danger for the eager and ambitious. As I have said, one becomes overidentified with his vocational role. So not only does one become overidentified with his role but that role gets idealized. So not only is one the founder-entrepreneur of the company, but if the company goes bankrupt, he may commit suicide.

If the line between me as person and me as careerist is not clearly drawn, I am a tree whose sap has run out, whose roots have rotted, and I am wood turning to stone.

It isn't the specific expectations of others that cause me to identify and idealize a role that is impossible for me to live up to.

It is *my* insistence, my commitment to succeed and obtain a few badges of belonging in order to gain entrance into some society of man I deem important.

I don't need to agonize over whether I need the approval of significant others. For me that debate is settled.

No man is an island, etc.

Only geniuses and psychotics can get along without the approval of others.

Actually, I'm not so sure about geniuses . . .

. . . and psychotics become psychotic because they never won the approval they needed.

For me, the essential discovery is who are the significant others that I really want to be a part of, belong to, and with whom I can carry my weight.

When I choose them, I will no longer have to ask the question whether what I am doing is conforming or being responsible.

If what I am doing is more drudgery than urgency, more dullness than excitement, more sapping than refreshing, then I am where what I give isn't liked and what I like isn't given.

But the *where* isn't a place.

It is an attitude.

Fish know nothing of water. A *New Yorker* cartoon shows two fish getting ashore: "This is where the action is!"

—Marshall McLuhan

I'm not denying that I can get caught up in a sick system that will not allow for human creativity, and my only self-respecting choice will be to get out.

But as in the case of the copping-out executives, I suspect most of my depression, when it occurs, comes from unimaginative capitulation to the dull mechanics of my role.

Somewhere *in* my role, if I am alive to myself I will find a natural flow to my actions, an outlet for that wellspring churning inside.

If I will chip away the crusty layers of routinized thinking I am certain to discover something fresh I am excited about; that others around me whom I haven't noticed also will find contagious and useful.

Sense-able is response-able.

It is not marching to the beat of a different drummer as much as it is drumming the beat to different marchers.

A wise company doesn't merely ask what is *the* market; it finds its niche by taking account of itself and asking, "What is *our* market?"

So it is with me when I'm authentic. I can bend, but I'm not molten. I do best and most enjoy what I do naturally and spontaneously.

And in all of life, not just my job, if I look hard enough, I can find the rhythm, the inner flow that generates constructive action toward and among my significant others.

In

    work,

        love

           and friendship . . .

my roles become what I seize within them.

A flower stretches for the sunlight . . .

I can learn from this.

Is it so small a thing
To have enjoy'd the sun,
To have lived light in the spring,
To have loved, to have thought, to have done;
To have advanced true friends,
   and beat down baffling foes?

                    —Matthew Arnold

ABOUT THE AUTHOR

Allan J. Cox is an organizational consultant and executive recruiter. He is President of the Chicago consulting firm Management Organization, Inc. A graduate of Northern Illinois University with a B.A. in social science and a Master's degree in sociology, Mr. Cox was an Associate Consultant with Case and Company and Spencer Stuart & Associates, and Vice President of Westcott Associates, before founding his own firm in 1969.

Before entering the business world, Mr. Cox was an instructor in sociology at Wheaton College for a period of three years. He holds professional memberships in The American Sociological Association; The American Group Psychotherapy Association; The American Society of Adlerian Psychology and Alpha Kappa Delta, the national sociology honor society.

At various times in the past, he has served on the boards of the Chicago chapter of The Academy of Religion and Mental Health; The John Howard Association of Illinois; The Illinois Council on Family Relations and the Chicago Center for Urban Projects.

He is married, the father of a seven-year-old daughter and makes his home on Chicago's near north side.